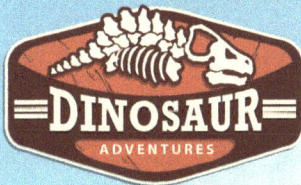

DINOSAUR
ADVENTURES

Get to Know
Dinosaurs

Alexis Roumanis

Explore other books at:
WWW.ENGAGEBOOKS.COM

VANCOUVER, B.C.

WWW.ENGAGEBOOKS.COM

Get to Know Dinosaurs: Level 1
Roumanis, Alexis 1982
Text © 2021 Engage Books

Edited by: Lauren Dick

Text set in Arial Regular.
Chapter headings set in Arial Black.

FIRST EDITION / FIRST PRINTING

LIBRARY AND ARCHIVES CANADA CATALOGUING IN PUBLICATION

Title: Get to know dinosaurs / Alexis Roumanis.
Names: Roumanis, Alexis, author.
Description: Series statement: Dinosaur adventures

Identifiers: Canadiana (print) 20210250151 | Canadiana (ebook) 20210250291
ISBN 978-1-77476-421-3 (hardcover)
ISBN 978-1-77476-422-0 (softcover)
ISBN 978-1-77476-423-7 (pdf)
ISBN 978-1-77476-424-4 (epub)
ISBN 978-1-77476-425-1 (audio)

Subjects:
LCSH: Readers
LCSH: Readers—Dinosaurs.

Classification: LCC PE1117 .D56 2021 | DDC J428.6—DC23

Contents

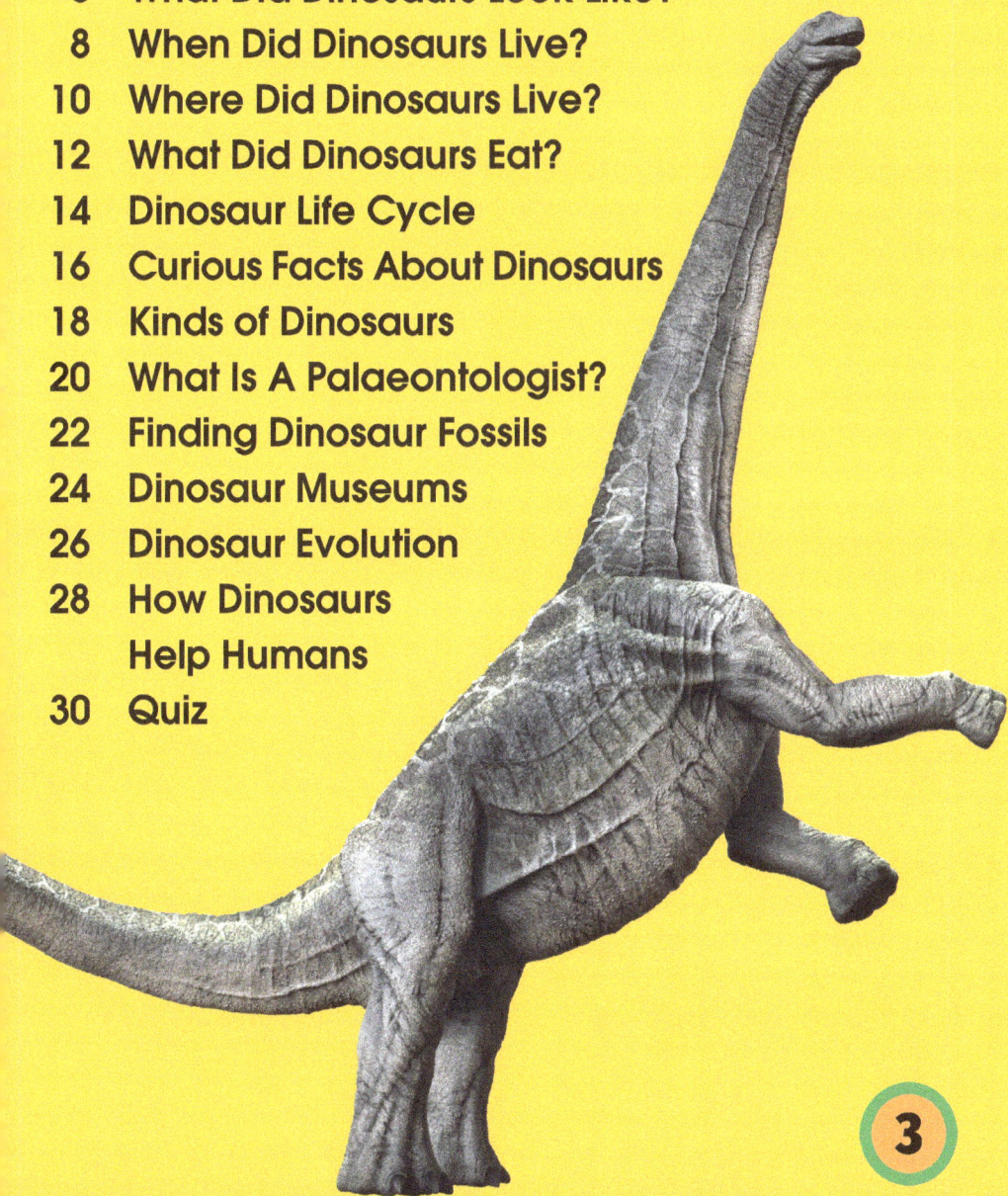

What Are Dinosaurs?

Dinosaurs are **reptiles**. The word dinosaur means "terrible lizard."

Reptiles are cold-blooded animals. They use heat from the Sun to stay warm.

What Did Dinosaurs Look Like?

Dinosaurs walked on two or four legs. They all had tails. The smallest dinosaur was about the size of a chicken. The largest dinosaurs were bigger than some schools.

The nails on a Triceratops (*tri-serra-tops*) are called hooves. Some dinosaurs had claws.

Horns and spikes helped to keep dinosaurs safe.

Spikes

Horns

Some dinosaurs had beaks just like birds.

When Did Dinosaurs Live?

Dinosaurs were the main animals on Earth for about 200 million years.

A large meteor hit Earth about 65 million years ago. Scientists think this is what killed most dinosaurs.

Where Did Dinosaurs Live?

Dinosaurs lived in the Mesozoic Era. Earth looked very different at the beginning of the Mesozoic. There was one large area of land called Pangea.

Pangea

Tethys Sea

Panthalassic Ocean

All around Pangea was the Panthalassic Ocean. Over time, Pangea started to break apart.

At the end of the Mesozoic, Earth looked similar to how it looks today. Tyrannosaurus Rex (T-Rex) (*tie-ran-oh-sore-us*), Velociraptor (*vel-oss-ee-rap-tor*), and Brachiosaurus (*brak-ee-oh-sore-us*) lived in different areas on Earth.

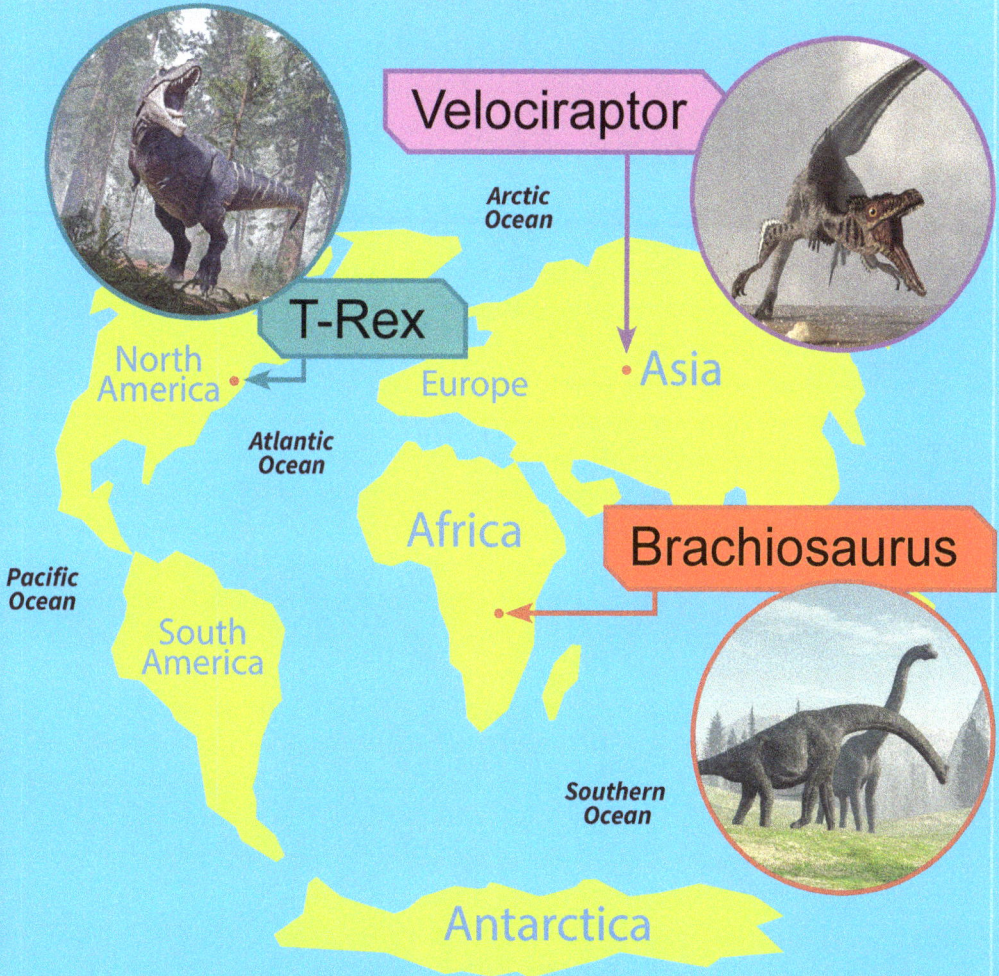

Velociraptor

T-Rex

Arctic Ocean

North America

Europe

Asia

Atlantic Ocean

Africa

Brachiosaurus

Pacific Ocean

South America

Southern Ocean

Antarctica

0   2,000 miles

0   4,000 kilometers (km)

N

Legend
Land
Ocean

What Did Dinosaurs Eat?

Dinosaurs ate mostly meat or plants. Meat eating dinosaurs are called carnivores. Plant eating dinosaurs are herbivores.

The Brachiosaurus' long neck helps it to eat leaves on tall trees.

Dinosaur Life Cycle

All dinosaurs hatch from eggs.

Baby dinosaurs are called hatchlings.

Young dinosaurs
are called juveniles.

T-Rex could live for about 30 years.
But, large plant-eating dinosaurs
lived for about 80 years.

Curious Facts About Dinosaurs

Argentinosaurus (*ar-gent-eeno-sore-us*) weighed more than 17 elephants. It may be the largest land animal to have ever lived.

Stegosaurus (*steg-oh-sore-us*) had a brain the size of a walnut.

Most herbivores had spikes and horns to help protect themselves.

Some dinosaurs had feathers.

Pteranodon (*teh-ran-o-don*) are not dinosaurs. They were flying reptiles that lived during the age of dinosaurs.

Humans have found more than 700 kinds of dinosaurs so far.

Kinds of Dinosaurs

Parasaurolophus (*pa-ra-saw-rol-off-us*) had large head crests they used to make trumpeting sounds.

Dilophosaurus (*die-loaf-oh-sore-us*) was one of the first large meat-eating dinosaurs.

Sauroposeidon (*sore-oh-poh-sigh-don*) was the tallest dinosaur. It was 59 feet (18 meters) tall.

Tyrannosaurus Rex was about the size of a school bus.

Stegosaurus had spikes that helped protect it from carnivores.

Velociraptor could run at speeds of about 40 miles (64 km) per hour.

Spinosaurus (*spine-oh-sore-us*) was a good swimmer, and ate fish.

What Is A Palaeontologist?

Palaeontologists study plants and animals that lived millions of years ago.

Palaeontologists study the remains of these living things. The remains are called fossils.

Finding Dinosaur Fossils

Palaeontologists look for fossils all over the world. They use special tools to dig for fossils.

Sometimes, palaeontologists will even find dinosaur footprints.

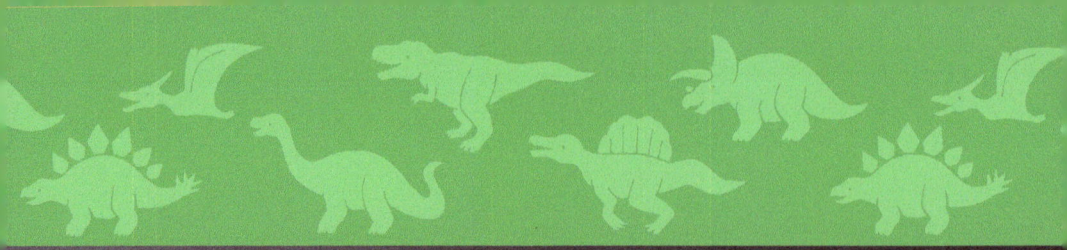

Dinosaur Museums

Some dinosaur fossils are pieced together like a puzzle. People can see them in a dinosaur museum.

Seeing dinosaurs at a museum can be exciting. It is a great way to learn more about dinosaurs and how they lived.

Dinosaur Evolution

Over time, dinosaurs changed in shape and size. This is called evolution.

T-Rex evolved from a dinosaur that was the size of a human child.

Protoceratops (*pro-toe-ker-ah-tops*) had no horns. It lived 2 million years before triceratops. Protoceratops evolved into triceratops.

Protoceratops

Triceratops had three horns.

How Dinosaurs Help Humans

Over time, Earth gets warmer and cooler. This is called climate change.

Only ten thousand years ago, Earth was mostly covered in ice and snow.

Paleontologists study how climate change affected dinosaurs. This helps them understand how climate change affects animals today.

Quiz

Test your knowledge of dinosaurs by answering the following questions. The questions are based on what you have read in this book. The answers are listed on the bottom of the next page.

1 What does the word dinosaur mean?

2 When did a large meteor hit Earth?

3 What was Pangea?

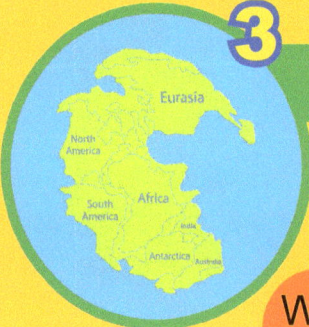

4 What are meat-eating dinosaurs called?

5 What are baby dinosaurs called?

6 What remains do palaeontologists dig for?

Explore Our Engage Books Readers!

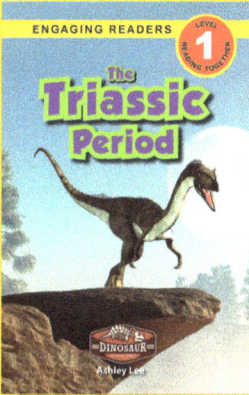

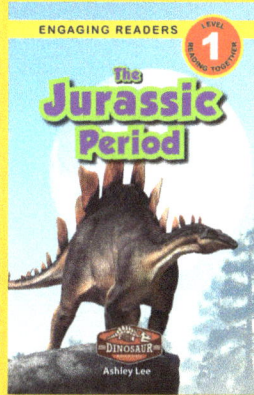

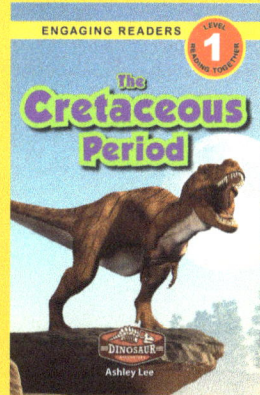

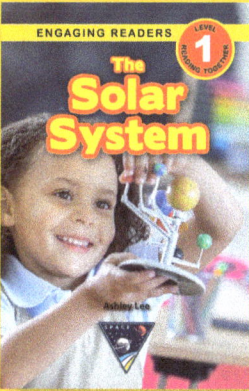

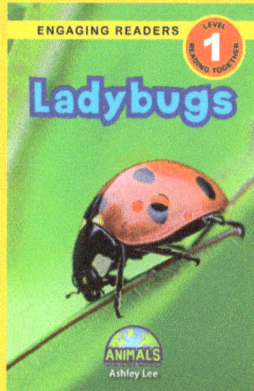

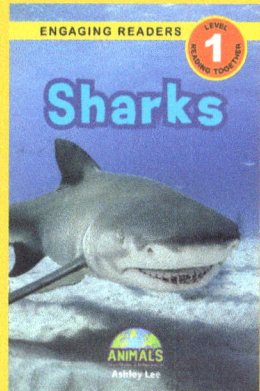

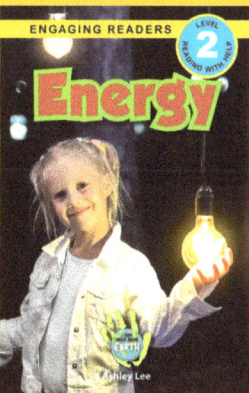

Visit www.engagebooks.com to explore more Engaging Readers.

Answers: 1. Terrible lizard 2. 65 million years ago 3. One large area of land 4. Carnivores 5. Hatchlings 6. Fossils

www.ingramcontent.com/pod-product-compliance
Lightning Source LLC
Chambersburg PA
CBHW051236020426
42331CB00016B/3402